Mick Hume is the editor of *Livin*

THE COMMUNIST MANIFESTO

THE COMMUNIST MANIFESTO

**Karl Marx
and
Frederick Engels**

Introduction by Mick Hume

junius

Pluto Press

London ● Chicago, Illinois

This edition first published 1996 by Junius Publications Ltd
BCM JPLtd, London WC1N 3XX
and Pluto Press
345 Archway Road, London N6 5AA
1436 West Randolph, Chicago, Illinois, 60607, USA

Translation by Samuel Moore, first published 1888
Introduction copyright © Junius Publications Ltd, 1996

British Library Cataloguing in Publication Data
A catalogue record for this book is available from the British Library

ISBN 0 7453 1034 6

Produced for Pluto Press by

Series coordinator
Peter Ray

Design
Richard Stead

Production
Alec Campbell, Andy Clarkson

Contents

Introduction

The Communist Manifesto is now almost 150 years old. It would be hard to think of any other slim volume which has been subjected to such constant and comprehensive criticism for almost a century and a half. So how has the *Manifesto* stood the test of time? What, if anything, does this little classic of the mid-nineteenth century have to offer us today, in the last years of the twentieth?

It is ironic that one of the major problems with the discussion of the *Manifesto* is that anti-Marxist commentators tend to accord it too much historic importance. It is often treated as the last word on Marxism, as if it contained a full exposition of Karl Marx's approach to the world. From this standpoint, if any part of the *Manifesto* can be put to question (albeit with the benefit of 150 years' worth of hindsight), then the whole of Marxism can be casually dumped in the dustbin of history. For if the *Manifesto* is indeed what the British historian AJP Taylor typically called it—'a holy book',[1] some kind of bible of Marxism—then any flaw in its argument which can be spotted by close scrutiny must surely cast doubt on the credibility of the entire Marxist doctrine.

That is one reason why the critics have often gathered around any scrap of the *Manifesto* which they believe can be challenged in the court of history. See, for example, how often the *Manifesto's* brief statement that 'the modern labourer...sinks deeper and deeper below the conditions of existence of his own class. He becomes a pauper' has been held up as 'proof' that Marxism cannot be right, since most workers in the advanced capitalist societies do not appear to have starved to death over the past 150 years.

---

1   AJP Taylor, 'Introduction', *The Communist Manifesto,* Penguin Classics, 1985, p7

Leaving aside for a moment the specific arguments raised in such narrow criticisms, this entire approach to *The Communist Manifesto* misses the point. The *Manifesto* is not a bible of Marxism (indeed there is no such thing). Nor is it in any sense a fully matured or complete exposition of the Marxist approach to politics, poverty or anything else.

Rather than crediting the *Manifesto* with such a bogus status, it would be more appropriate to view it as the equivalent of an election leaflet; or perhaps as the contemporary version of what would now be a televised party political broadcast. The document's proper name is *Manifesto of the Communist Party* (even though no party of that name existed at the time of publication). It was written not as a testament for posterity, but as a propagandist intervention in the specific debates and issues of a turbulent moment in European history, on the eve of the revolutionary upsurge of 1848. In dashing off the *Manifesto* between December 1847 and January 1848, Marx's aim was not to leave a timeless philosophical legacy to the world, but to give direction to the political ferment of the day.

Seen in this light, it becomes much easier to assess the *Manifesto* in a more balanced fashion. It certainly displays all of the limitations of an election manifesto—a hastily written piece which contains some half-formulated arguments alongside some powerful insights, and addresses some specific issues of the day which quickly passed into insignificance or oblivion. The *Manifesto's* substance can in no way be compared to the breadth and depth of the systematic works of Marx, which were produced over the subsequent 35 years. Those who want to be taken seriously as critics of Marxism would surely do better to take on the weighty theoretical challenge thrown down by the three volumes of Marx's greatest work, *Capital*, than to waste time picking little holes in the 40 or so pages of *The Communist Manifesto*, written by a 29-year old Karl Marx with the support of the 27-year old Frederick Engels.

Marx and Engels themselves were under no illusions as to the historic status of *The Communist Manifesto*. In their preface to the 1872 German edition, they pointed out that the important developments of the previous 24 years had already rendered parts of the *Manifesto* redundant, especially the list of specific demands at the end of Section 2 and the Section 3 polemics against other socialist parties which had

Introduction

long since ceased to exist. In particular Marx and Engels drew attention to the development of their own political outlook following the bitter experience of the 1871 Paris Commune, which had proved that 'the working class cannot simply lay hold of the ready-made state machinery and wield it for its own purposes', but must break the power of the state machine and replace it with a state of its own.

Those critics who think it a clever insight to point out that things have changed since 1848 might note, then, that Marx and Engels were way ahead of them, having made the point about the *Manifesto* falling behind the times well over a century ago. The authors felt no compunction to rewrite their old text in order to take account of these changes, concluding instead that 'the *Manifesto* has become a historical document which we have no longer any right to alter'—any more than the political parties of today have the right to go back and rewrite their manifestos for the last election, or newspaper editors the right to alter the leader article they published last week.

The *Manifesto* was written as a propagandist intervention in an immediate political conflict, rather than the complete philosophical treatise which it is often treated as today. Notwithstanding that qualification, however, *The Communist Manifesto* remains worthy of attention, and as something more than a historical artefact. The often embryonic ideas contained in the *Manifesto* do lay bare many of the key workings of and tensions within capitalist society—tensions which have only been heightened by the intervening years. The Russian revolutionary Leon Trotsky, writing in 1937, considered that the pamphlet displayed 'greater genius than any other in world literature', thanks to the way in which 'the young authors...were able to look further into the future than anyone before them, and perhaps than anyone since them'.[2]

If Marx and Engels had been able to see far enough into the future to study the intellectual temper of our times, they would have found a mood of profound pessimism and gloom about the way that the advance of industry, science and technology over the past two centuries has allegedly damaged human life and the natural environment. By contrast, *The Communist Manifesto* of 1848 was keen to uphold and even to celebrate the achievements of capitalism in overcoming and controlling nature for the good of humanity, through the rapid development of industry, science, agriculture, and telecommunications.

The bourgeoisie or capitalist class, declared the *Manifesto*, 'has been

---

2   L Trotsky, 'Ninety years of *The Communist Manifesto*', in *New International*, February 1938

the first to show what man's activity can bring about'. Within a century it had 'accomplished wonders far surpassing Egyptian pyramids, Roman aqueducts, and Gothic cathedrals; it has conducted expeditions that put in the shade all former exoduses of nations and crusades'. Today the 'wonders' of bourgeois achievement, from the motor car to satellite television or genetic engineering, are more likely to be condemned as corrupters of nature than championed as liberators of humanity. It is a telling sign of the degree to which society's elites have lost faith in themselves and their system that they can no longer effectively defend the kind of capitalist gains which communists were keen to celebrate 150 years ago.

But the *Manifesto* is no advert for the market economy. Alongside its recognition of the expansive and universalising tendencies within capitalism, it also identifies the other side of the coin; the destructive tendencies which were powerful enough within capitalism then, but which, since Marx's time, have become the dominant characteristics of a stagnant system. Although Marx's analysis of the capitalist crisis would not be fully developed for another two decades, the *Manifesto* contains the bare bones of a critique of the system's operation.

'For many a decade past', notes Marx in the *Manifesto*, 'the history of industry and commerce is but the history of the revolt of modern productive forces against modern conditions of production, against the property relations that are the conditions for the existence of the bourgeoisie and of its rule'. Here Marx identified a key contradiction within capitalism: that between the dynamic towards increasing production, and the constraints imposed on production by the predominance of private property relations. These relations dictate that the goods and services which the whole of society needs can only be produced if the process is profitable to the minority of capitalists. The consequence of this contradiction, Marx noted, is that capitalism frequently experiences a crisis of production, in the form of a recession. The world economy has been transformed beyond recognition over the past century and a half. Yet, since the 1970s, the renewed experience of international economic slump has acted as a powerful rejoinder to those who had sought to dismiss as nonsense the *Manifesto's* suggestion that capitalist crises would grow more profound in the future.

At the heart of the *Manifesto's* argument against capitalism is the subjugation of the working class—those who have to survive by selling their ability to work for an employer. Despite the much-noted disappearance of cloth caps, and the advent of 'luxuries' like mass home ownership and holidays abroad, the vast majority of people in Western societies still fit into the category of worker thanks to their relationship with capital. The *Manifesto* outlined how the fair exchange of the capitalist labour market disguises the process of exploitation; how the worker is paid the value of his labour-power, only for the capitalist to appropriate the surplus which that labour-power produces when put to work. Alienated from the product of his labour, the worker becomes, in the words of the *Manifesto*, 'an appendage of the machine'. The fact that the machine today is more likely to be a PC or a supermarket checkout than a mill loom or an iron smelter cannot alter the fundamentally dehumanising reality of that experience. The *Manifesto's* identification of the need to overthrow the existing social relations in order to liberate the majority of society has surely stood the test of time.

But so what? might come the answer from the cynical late 1990s. It is all very well, the critics of today would say, to identify shortcomings with the capitalist mode of production. But Marx's arguments are empty if there is no alternative, if it is not possible to change the way society is organised for the better. And the experience of the past 150 years is now widely taken as proof that the attempt to change society is at best a utopian dream, and at worst paves the way to a totalitarian nightmare.

This is the nub of the argument so far as the *Manifesto's* relevance to the present is concerned. Marx and Engels' work sets out a powerful case for change; Section 1 of the *Manifesto* outlines the materialist approach to the process of historical change, while much of Section 2 is devoted to a funny and biting response to the bourgeois objections to change. The argument for understanding and embracing historical and social change is at the heart of the *Manifesto;* and it remains the *Manifesto's* major legacy. The case for change needs to be restated in contemporary terms today, at a time when the issue has been effectively removed from the political agenda.

The certainty with which Marx expressed his faith in the future in the *Manifesto*—'The proletarians have nothing to lose but their chains. They have a world to win'—is now widely dismissed as dangerously naive. Society has experienced a profound disillusionment with the project of change. The apparent failure of every experiment with social change from the Soviet Union to the Western welfare state has hardened many hearts against further attempts. There is a disenchantment not just with radical political change, but with the old goals of 'progress' in every field of human endeavour: any breakthrough in medical science is now accompanied by immediate warnings about possible side-effects, any new technology raises automatic fears about environmental damage.

The pessimistic mood of anti-modernity now transcends the old left-right political divide. Herbert Marcuse personifies the consensus against 'progress'. Twenty years ago he was already arguing that 'intensified progress seems to be bound up with intensified unfreedom':

'Concentration camps, mass exterminations, world wars and atom bombs are no "relapse into barbarism", but the unrepressed implementation of the achievements of modern science, technology and domination. And the most effective subjugation of man by man takes place at the height of civilisation, when the material and intellectual attainment of mankind seem to allow the creation of a truly free world.' [3]

This influential outlook draws a more-or-less straight line leading from the Enlightenment of the seventeenth and eighteenth centuries, with its dream of untrammelled scientific and intellectual progress, to the Holocaust of the twentieth, with its death camp combination of technology and human arrogance.

The disillusionment with change has gathered pace in recent decades, as the impasse of capitalist society has coincided with the discrediting of the old alternatives. We have gone from Daniel Bell's 'End of ideology' thesis in the sixties, through Francis Fukuyama's 'End of history' argument at the end of the eighties, to a situation in which every fashionable theory is required to introduce itself with the prefix 'post-', denoting that, as one commentator puts it, 'we are past the new', and implying 'a belatedness, an age in which everything has always

---

3   H Marcuse, *Eros and Civilisation,* Abacus, 1972, p23

already occurred'.[4] The pessimistic, cynical and ultimately conservative climate of our times is perhaps best captured in the phrase which the British Conservative prime minister Margaret Thatcher made her own in the 1980s—'There is no alternative'. In the Reagan-Thatcher era, that was a ringing assertion of the supremacy of free market economics. Now, by contrast, it amounts to a resigned acknowledgement that, while the market may have its problems and require some regulation, it is the best that we can hope for.

The general disenchantment with the experience of change also points up a specific refutation of Karl Marx's view of history. An impressive range of heavyweight critics—FA Hayek, JH Plumb, JA Hall, Allan Bloom and many more—can be lined up to criticise Marx's work, from the *Manifesto* onwards, for allegedly insisting that historical progress was 'inevitable'. Marx is constantly accused of holding a deterministic, mechanical view of history, in which civilisation advances as if by numbers from slavery through feudalism to capitalism and then communism, with humanity forever moving onwards and upwards on the unstoppable tide of Progress.

Warming to their theme, some critics go so far as to accuse Marx of acting like a religious prophet prophesying the Second Coming, with History or Progress having taken the place of the Messiah as the force from without which would inevitably come to the salvation of mankind. So the American Allan Bloom announces that 'Marx denied the existence of God but turned over all His functions to history, which is inevitably directed to a goal fulfilling of man and which takes the place of Providence'.[5] In his widely read 1967 introduction to *The Communist Manifesto*, AJP Taylor refers to Marx as 'a prophet, not a philosopher', and says that the *Manifesto* contains the elements which made Marxism 'the last and most contemporary of the great religions':

---

4   B Thomas, 'The New Historicism', quoted in F Füredi, *Mythical Past, Elusive Future: History and Society in an Anxious Age*, Pluto Press, 1992, p217. See also D Bell, *The End of Ideology: On the Exhaustion of Political Ideas in the Fifties*, Free Press, 1964; F Fukuyama, *The End of History and the Last Man*, Hamish Hamilton, 1992

5   A Bloom, *The Closing of the American Mind: How Higher Education Has Failed Democracy and Impoverished the Souls of Today's Students*, Penguin, 1988, p196

'[Marx] was convinced that events moved always towards the victory of the Higher. This faith in the inevitable outcome made him a great religious teacher. The inevitable rarely happens in real life.'[6]

Taylor's parting shot was an easy one. After all, society has not developed in the way that Marx wanted it to, capitalism has not been superseded by communism. And if he said that progressive change was inevitable, and it has not come about, he must surely have been totally wrong. This observation, that the goals first set out in the *Manifesto* have never been achieved, remains the central piece of hard evidence in the orthodox case against the Marxist view of historical change.

It is certainly true that, for reasons which would take volumes to explain, the aspirations for emancipation which the *Manifesto* expressed have never fully been realised. It is also true that the odd specific expectation expressed by Marx and Engels' pamphlet never came to pass; for instance, the German democratic revolution of 1848 did not prove to be 'the prelude to an immediately following proletarian revolution'. But it is equally certain that Marx would not have been shocked or unnerved by these developments. For while words like 'inevitable', 'uniform' or 'unilinear' are continually employed by critics of the Marxist view of history, they are noticeable by their absence in Marx's own works. The materialist conception of history, discovered by Marx only a short time before he applied it in writing the *Manifesto*, explicitly rejects all such notions of inevitability in regard to progress.

No doubt the critics would respond by pointing to one statement in the *Manifesto*, at the very end of Section 1, where Marx suggests that the fall of the bourgeoisie and the victory of the proletariat 'are equally inevitable'. But that flourish was simply the typical rhetoric of an agitational pamphlet, designed to impress upon Marx's intended audience that they could win. All of the substantial theoretical work he produced over the following decades made clear his rejection of any fatalistic view of history. Singling out that one statement from the *Manifesto* as the essence of Marxism is a crass example of how the critics choose to inflate the status of this pamphlet, and demand standards of Marx's propaganda that they would not apply to others.

---

6   'Introduction', *The Communist Manifesto*, p7

After all, how many party leaders or speechwriters have *not* declared that victory was assured on the eve of battle? If such rhetorical flourishes were always considered a capital offence (as they seem to be when employed by Marx), bourgeois politics would have died out from want of candidates long ago.

The fact is that from the writing of *The German Ideology* (five years before the *Manifesto*) onwards, Marx and Engels argued against general theories of history. Marx insisted that all events had to be understood in their specific historical and social context, and that there was no ready-made model or 'master key' with which to interpret the historical process. He was resolutely against prophesies and all expressions of pseudo-religious faith in 'progress'. Indeed Marx directly rejected any notion of an inevitable, ever upwards course of human advance: 'In spite of the pretensions of "Progress"', wrote Marx, 'continual retrogressions and circular movements occur...the category "Progress" is completely empty and abstract.'[7]

If Marx is not guilty of the charge of religiosity, then what is his case for historical change? The first line of Section 1 of the *Manifesto* gives a major hint: 'The history of all hitherto existing societies is the history of class struggles.' This often-quoted (and nearly as often misunderstood) phrase is not meant to suggest that history has been one long miners' strike. Instead, it makes clear Marx's view that there has been no predetermined course to human history. It has not been dictated by God, or by the 'eternal truths' beloved of the bourgeoisie. History has been made by men and women, through a process of struggle; a struggle fought out in different times and circumstances, but always in pursuit of conflicting material interests between the ruling classes and the ruled, the exploiters and the exploited. It is this struggle which has driven human society and its productive forces forwards, in fits and starts, over thousands of years.

In mapping out the development of the modern class struggle between the bourgeois and the proletarians in the *Manifesto*, Marx is first at pains to emphasise that 'the bourgeoisie, historically, has played a most revolutionary part' in breaking down the old feudal and patriarchal order, and transforming every aspect of production and society

---

7   K Marx and F Engels, *Collected Works*, Vol4, Lawrence & Wishart, 1975, p83

beyond recognition. Marx's backhanded compliment to the bourgeoisie here acts as a pointed reminder that those who now dismiss the
argument for historical and social change were once the harbingers of it
themselves; it was only once it had become the ruling class that the
revolutionary bourgeoisie was converted to the cause of conservatism
and reaction.

And just as, at a certain point of history, the bourgeoisie arose out of
the pre-capitalist order and fought to free itself from the fetters of the
ancien régime, so the *Manifesto* points out that capitalism has given
birth to 'its own gravediggers', the working class, who would have to
struggle to change society once more in pursuit of their material interests. The difference being that, for the first time in history, the struggle
would be to create a society organised in the interests of the majority
rather than those of a property-owning minority. 'In place of the old
bourgeois society, with its classes and class antagonisms', declares the
Manifesto, 'we shall have an association, in which the free development
of each is the condition for the free development of all'.

None of this, however, should be seen as in any sense inevitable.
Marx's materialist conception of history does not suggest that men and
women can simply shape their destinies in any way which suits them.
It argues instead that humanity has the *potential* to make its own
history. How that potential is realised in practice will always depend
upon the complex interaction of material circumstances and society's
consciousness in any specific context. The struggle for change is itself in
a constant process of change and flux, to-and-fro.

The fact that Marx rejected any notion of historical inevitability is
evidenced by his concentration on the question of consciousness—the
subjective outlook of those struggling for emancipation. He understood that, in the words of the *Manifesto,* 'the ruling ideas of each age
have ever been the ideas of its ruling class', and that the proletariat
would require the utmost clarity and awareness of its own position and
latent power if it was to counter ruling class ideology and realise its
revolutionary potential. He saw the task of communists as being to
provide that clarity and direction. As we have noted, *The Communist
Manifesto* itself was an early propagandist attempt to intervene in
and direct the struggles of its day. And Marx and Engels were to fight
a constant battle of ideas as events developed over the following

decades. As they noted in their 1872 preface, the 'general principles' of the *Manifesto* might still hold good, but 'the practical application of the principles will depend, as the *Manifesto* itself states, everywhere and at all times on the historical conditions for the time being existing'.

If Marx had truly believed that the triumph of socialism was inevitable, why on Earth would he have bothered slaving to write the *Manifesto* as an intervention in the struggle for change? And why would he have spent the next 35 years trying to evolve and sharpen the 'general principles' of Marxism in order always to advance the cause of revolution in 'the historical conditions for the time being existing'? Marx believed , as he said elsewhere, that men make their own history, but not in circumstances of their own choosing. In the revolutionary circumstances of 1848, he sought through the *Manifesto* to convince Europeans that they had an opportunity to make history. In the event, however, the historical development of capitalism and of communist politics was not to favour the proletarian revolution for another 70 years.

Much of the confusion over Marx's attitude towards historical progress centres on the status of the human subject. Many commentators today acknowledge that major economic and political changes still take place in the world. But they tend to see these changes as spontaneous, external events, beyond the control of governments or any other human agency; see, for instance, the fashionable preoccupation with the 'globalisation' of world financial markets, or the influence of the laws of 'chaos'. A common theme in all of these discussions is that humanity is reduced to the object of change, a bystander to which things happen. For Marx, by contrast, as the *Manifesto's* line about all history being of class struggles indicates, the one constant in the changing process of history was the status of humanity as the historical subject—the potential maker of history. The subjective factor of human action and struggle is central to shaping events. Once that is grasped (along with the simple fact that the outcome of a struggle can go either way) it should be clear that the materialist concept of historical change is neither mechanical nor deterministic. Remove that understanding of the human subject, however, and problems arise.

Conservative critics of Marx have always sought to emphasise the weight of tradition and continuity with the past, to depict the present social arrangements as the natural order of things, and to play down the potential of people to define their own futures. In recent times, however, events have conspired to spread doubt about humanity's history-making potential throughout society. For a variety of reasons (not least the demise of the old working class movement of which Marx witnessed the birth), the predominant experience of people today is that of atomised, powerless individuals. They are more likely to feel themselves to be passive victims—of crime, unemployment or some other threat—rather than active shapers of their destiny. From such a perspective in which humanity is relegated to the status of an object rather than the subject of history, the materialist approach of the *Manifesto* can readily be twisted into its opposite—a religious philosophy—as Frank Füredi has explained:

> 'Once the role of human history-making is suppressed, it is possible to treat the subject mechanistically...history stands external to society. It imposes its dictates on the passive individual....Interpreted from this perspective, that is one where there is no historical subject, Marx's view of history can be readily transformed into a religion.'[8]

Once the historical subject is removed from the picture, it also becomes possible for the critics of change quoted above to associate progress with the horrors of the twentieth century. Divorced from the concept of human struggle, 'progress' becomes simply the passage of time, and can be blamed for anything new that happens—including the creation of death camps and Holocausts which in reality were intended to hold back human progress and liberation.

The role of the human subject in the process of history-making is at the heart of *The Communist Manifesto's* message; indeed the *Manifesto* itself was written to make the proletariat aware of its historic potential to change the world. In the atmosphere of today, however, when the tendency is always to diminish the scope for humanity to take action and take control, the subject has been removed from the picture—and even *The Communist Manifesto* has been recruited to the cause of

---

8 F Füredi, *Mythical Past, Elusive Future: History and Society in an Anxious Age*, Pluto Press, 1992, pp264-65

conservatism. Assorted pundits and business analysts have been heard to quote Marx's famous statement that 'all that is solid melts into air', in order to illustrate their contention that the world is beyond human comprehension or control. In fact those who bother to read the *Manifesto* will find that the passage concerned is about how the advent of capitalism raises the possibility of people taking control of their destiny, as it strips the veils and prejudices of the old order, so that 'man is at last compelled to face, with sober senses, his real conditions of life and his relations with his kind'.

Whatever else we might think of *The Communist Manifesto*'s relevance to today, there is a pressing need to reassert its message concerning the role of the human subject in historical and social change. People need not be powerless prisoners of the past; they have the potential to be active makers of their history, to make the world in their own image as the the *Manifesto* puts it. Winning that argument in the face of the contemporary culture of cynicism and low horizons is the precondition for challenging the politics of Tina—There is no alternative.

One important lesson to be learned from the *Manifesto* is that, however it is posed, an argument against the possibility of people changing the way society is run is ultimately an apologetic defence of the status quo. In the *Manifesto*, Marx ridicules all of the religious, moral and economic arguments ranged against the communists—such as the notion that they wanted to make women common property—and exposes these high-minded objections as nothing more than the propaganda devices of the bourgeoisie. Today, the widespread sentiment against social change may not be consciously motivated by a similar desire to defend capitalism. But its apologetic content and consequence are the same. Those who reject the possibility of change can only end up, whether implicitly or explicitly, as a friend of Tina. It is time that somebody did for the cynics of our time what Marx did for the critics of his, and revealed the dangerous assumptions underpinning their arguments. The current sense of terminus rests upon a low opinion of the potential capabilities of the humanity of which we are all a part. In practice, disparaging the human potential and removing the human subject from history means rejecting any responsibility for determining our own future.

The Communist Manifesto is not a bible to be repeated by rote or an icon to be worshipped uncritically. In many ways its specific arguments are outdated and irrelevant to our times. Developing a critique of capitalism relevant to the end of the twentieth century certainly demands that we go beyond what Marx said in the middle of the nineteenth. But that will only be possible if we learn to make the most of the powerful *method* of analysis which Marx developed, and which *The Communist Manifesto* gives a glimpse of.

Those who seek casually to dismiss Marxism as an authoritarian dogma which belongs in the past, and to uphold the 'individuality and freedom' of the market system, would do well to dwell upon the *Manifesto's* description of the difference between the status of the individual and his labour in a capitalist and a communist society. Having established that capital is but the accumulated product of the labour of the past, Marx put his attackers straight on the matter of who is on the side of the present or the past, the living or the dead:

'In bourgeois society, living labour is but a means to increase accumulated labour. In communist society, accumulated labour is but a means to widen, to enrich, to promote the existence of the labourer.

'In bourgeois society, therefore, the past dominates the present; in communist society, the present dominates the past. In bourgeois society capital is independent and has individuality, while the living person is dependent and has no individuality.

'And the abolition of this state of things is called by the bourgeois, abolition of individuality and freedom!'

Contrary to the caricatures produced over the past 150 years, Marx was the truest supporter of individuality and freedom. As the *Manifesto* suggests, however, he understood that the exercise of genuine individuality and freedom for all would depend upon the creation of a world in which people could make conscious choices about their lives, free from the constraints imposed by the power of capital and what the *Manifesto* calls 'the bourgeois claptrap' about moral codes and family values. In 1848 the young Marx had already glimpsed that the potential to create such a world lay in the hands of the disenfranchised workers, if they could be armed with the politics of social revolution. He saw his job as arming them through an open battle of ideas, with *The Communist Manifesto* as ammunition. 'The communists disdain to conceal their views and aims', he wrote at its conclusion, 'They openly declare that their ends can be attained only by the forcible overthrow of all existing social conditions'.

When AJP Taylor said, in his introduction to the *Manifesto*, that Marx was 'a prophet, not a philosopher', he was half-right. Marx was not a philosopher; as Engels said at his death, he was above all 'a revolutionist'. Or as Marx himself put it, in the famous quote from the *Theses on Feuerbach* that is inscribed on the monstrous gravestone in Highgate Cemetery: 'The philosophers have only *interpreted* the world, in various ways; the point is to *change* it.' *The Communist Manifesto* was written as a means to that end in the circumstances of its time. Whatever its limitations, we could well do with its equivalent for today.

Preface to the
German edition of 1872

The Communist League, an international association of workers, which could of course be only a secret one under the conditions obtaining at the time, commissioned the undersigned, at the Congress held in London in November 1847, to draw up for publication a detailed theoretical and practical programme of the party. Such was the origin of the following manifesto, the manuscript of which travelled to London, to be printed, a few weeks before the February Revolution.[1] First published in German, it has been republished in that language in at least 12 different editions in Germany, England and America. It was published in English for the first time in 1850 in the *Red Republican*, London, translated by Miss Helen Macfarlane, and in 1871 in at least three different translations in America. A French version first appeared in Paris shortly before the June insurrection of 1848[2] and recently in *Le Socialiste* of New York. A new translation is in the course of preparation. A Polish version appeared in London shortly after it was first published in German. A Russian translation was published in Geneva in the sixties. Into Danish, too, it was translated shortly after its first appearance.

However much the state of things may have altered during the last 25 years, the general principles laid down in this manifesto are, on the whole, as correct today as ever. Here and there some detail might be improved. The practical application of the principles will depend, as

---

1 The February Revolution—The overthrow of Louis Philippe in France, one of the uprisings that swept Europe in 1848 inspired by the ideals of the Great French Revolution of the 1790s.

2 The June insurrection—an uprising by Paris workers that was crushed by the republican regime.

the Manifesto itself states, everywhere and at all times, on the historical conditions for the time being existing, and, for that reason, no special stress is laid on the revolutionary measures proposed at the end of Section 2. That passage would, in many respects, be very differently worded today. In view of the gigantic strides of modern industry in the last 25 years, and of the accompanying improved and extended party organisation of the working class, in view of the practical experience gained, first in the February Revolution, and then, still more, in the Paris Commune, where the proletariat for the first time held political power for two whole months, this programme has in some details become antiquated. One thing especially was proved by the Commune, viz, that 'the working class cannot simply lay hold of the ready-made state machinery, and wield it for its own purposes' (see *The Civil War in France*, where this point is further developed).[3] Further, it is self-evident that the criticism of socialist literature is deficient in relation to the present time, because it comes down only to 1847; also that the remarks on the relation of the communists to the various opposition parties (Section 4), although in principle still correct, yet in practice are antiquated, because the political situation has been entirely changed, and the progress of history has swept from off the Earth the greater portion of the political parties there enumerated.

But, then, the *Manifesto* has become a historical document which we have no longer any right to alter. A subsequent edition may perhaps appear with an introduction bridging the gap from 1847 to the present day; this reprint was too unexpected to leave us time for that.

Karl Marx, Frederick Engels
London, 24 June 1872

---

3   The Paris Commune—following the defeat of Louis Bonaparte and the prolonged siege of Paris by German armies in 1870-71, the workers of Paris—defending the city after the ruling classes had run away—established the Commune, the world's first proletarian state. It survived for just 72 days before being crushed by the forces of the new capitalist government, based at Versailles, with German assistance. *The Civil War in France* contains Marx's analysis of the historic significance of the Commune.

Preface to the
German edition of 1883

The preface to the present edition I must, alas, sign alone. Marx—the man to whom the whole working class of Europe and America owes more than to anyone else—rests at Highgate Cemetery and over his grave the first grass is already growing. Since his death, there can be even less thought of revising or supplementing the *Manifesto*. All the more do I consider it necessary again to state here the following expressly:

The basic thought running through the *Manifesto*—that economic production and the structure of society of every historical epoch necessarily arising therefrom constitute the foundation for the political and intellectual history of that epoch; that consequently (ever since the dissolution of the primeval communal ownership of land) all history has been a history of class struggles, of struggles between exploited and exploiting, between dominated and dominating classes at various stages of social development; that this struggle, however, has now reached a stage where the exploited and oppressed class (the proletariat) can no longer emancipate itself from the class which exploits and oppresses it (the bourgeoisie), without at the same time for ever freeing the whole of society from exploitation, oppression and class struggles—this basic thought belongs solely and exclusively to Marx.

I have already stated this many times; but precisely now it is necessary that it also stand in front of the *Manifesto* itself.

Frederick Engels
London, 28 June 1883

Preface to the
German edition of 1890

Since the above was written,[1] a new German edition of the *Manifesto* has again become necessary, and much has also happened to the *Manifesto* which should be recorded here.

A second Russian translation—by Vera Zasulich—appeared at Geneva in 1882; the preface to that edition was written by Marx and myself. Unfortunately, the original German manuscript has gone astray; I must therefore retranslate from the Russian, which will in no way improve the text. It reads:

'The first Russian edition of the *Manifesto of the Communist Party*, translated by Bakunin, was published early in the sixties by the printing office of the *Kolokol*. Then the West could see in it (the Russian edition of the *Manifesto*) only a literary curiosity. Such a view would be impossible today.

'What a limited field the proletarian movement still occupied at that time (December 1847) is most clearly shown by the last section of the *Manifesto*: the position of the communists in relation to the various opposition parties in the various countries. Precisely Russia and the United States are missing here. It was the time when Russia constituted the last great reserve of all European reaction, when the United States absorbed the surplus proletarian forces of Europe through immigration. Both countries provided Europe with raw materials and were at the same time markets for the sale of its industrial products. At that time both were, therefore, in one way or another, pillars of the existing European order.

---

1   Engels is referring to his preface to the German edition of 1883.

'How very different today! Precisely European immigration fitted North America for a gigantic agricultural production, whose competition is shaking the very foundations of European landed property—large and small. In addition it enabled the United States to exploit its tremendous industrial resources with an energy and on a scale that must shortly break the industrial monopoly of Western Europe, and especially of England, existing up to now. Both circumstances react in revolutionary manner upon America itself. Step by step the small and middle landownership of the farmers, the basis of the whole political constitution, is succumbing to the competition of giant farms; simultaneously, a mass proletariat and a fabulous concentration of capitals are developing for the first time in the industrial regions.

'And now Russia! During the Revolution of 1848-49 not only the European princes, but the European bourgeois as well, found their only salvation from the proletariat, just beginning to awaken, in Russian intervention. The Tsar was proclaimed the chief of European reaction. Today he is a prisoner of war of the revolution, in Gatchina, and Russia forms the vanguard of revolutionary action in Europe.

'*The Communist Manifesto* had as its object the proclamation of the inevitably impending dissolution of modern bourgeois property. But in Russia we find, face to face with the rapidly developing capitalist swindle and bourgeois landed property, just beginning to develop, more than half the land owned in common by the peasants. Now the question is: can the Russian *obshchina*, though greatly undermined, yet a form of the primeval common ownership of land, pass directly to the higher form of communist common ownership? Or on the contrary, must it first pass through the same process of dissolution as constitutes the historical evolution of the West?

'The only answer to that possible today is this: if the Russian revolution becomes the signal for a proletarian revolution in the West, so that both complement each other, the present Russian common ownership of land may serve as the starting point for a communist development. (Karl Marx and Frederick Engels, London, 21 January 1882)

At about the same date, a new Polish version appeared in Geneva: *Manifest Komunistyczny*.

Furthermore, a new Danish translation has appeared in the *Social-demokratisk Bibliothek*, Copenhagen, 1885. Unfortunately it is not quite complete; certain essential passages, which seem to have presented difficulties to the translator, have been omitted, and in addition there are signs of carelessness here and there, which are all the more unpleasantly conspicuous since the translation indicates that had the translator taken a little more pains he would have done an excellent piece of work. A new French version appeared in 1885 in *Le Socialiste* of Paris; it is the best published to date.

From this latter a Spanish version was published the same year, first in *El Socialista* of Madrid, and then reissued in pamphlet form: *Manifiesto del Partido Comunista* por Carlos Marx y F Engels, Madrid, Administracion de *El Socialista*, Hernan Cortes 8.

As a matter of curiosity I may also mention that in 1887 the manuscript of an Armenian translation was offered to a publisher in Constantinople. But the good man did not have the courage to publish something bearing the name of Marx and suggested that the translator set down his own name as author, which the latter, however, declined.

After one and then another of the more or less inaccurate American translations had been repeatedly reprinted in England, an authentic version at last appeared in 1888. This was by my friend Samuel Moore, and we went through it together once more before it was sent to press. It is entitled: *Manifesto of the Communist Party*, by Karl Marx and Frederick Engels. Authorised English Translation, edited and annotated by Frederick Engels, 1888. London, William Reeves, 185 Fleet St, EC1 have added some of the notes of that edition to the present one.

The *Manifesto* has had a history of its own. Greeted with enthusiasm, at the time of its appearance, by the then still not at all numerous vanguard of scientific socialism (as is proved by the translations mentioned in the first preface), it was soon forced into the background by the reaction that began with the defeat of the Paris workers in June 1848, and was finally excommunicated 'according to law' by the conviction of the Cologne communists in November 1852. With the disappearance from the public scene of the workers movement that had begun with the February Revolution, the *Manifesto* too passed into the background.

When the working class of Europe had again gathered sufficient strength for a new onslaught upon the power of the ruling classes, the International Working Men's Association came into being. Its aim was to weld together into one huge army the whole militant working class of Europe and America. Therefore it could not set out from the principles laid down in the *Manifesto*. It was bound to have a programme which would not shut the door on the English trade unions, the French, Belgian, Italian and Spanish Proudhonists and the German Lassalleans[2] This programme, the preamble to the Rules of the International—was drawn up by Marx with a master hand acknowledged even by Bakunin and the anarchists. For the ultimate triumph of the ideas set forth in the *Manifesto* Marx relied solely and exclusively upon the intellectual development of the working class, as it necessarily had to ensue from united action and discussion. The events and vicissitudes in the struggle against capital, the defeats even more than the successes, could not but demonstrate to the fighters the inadequacy hitherto of their universal panaceas and make their minds more receptive to a thorough understanding of the true conditions for the emancipation of the workers. And Marx was right. The working class of 1874, at the dissolution of the International, was altogether different from that of 1864, at its foundation. Proudhonism in the Latin countries and the specific Lassalleanism in Germany were dying out, and even the then arch-conservative English trade unions were gradually approaching the point where in 1887 the chairman of their Swansea Congress could say in their name 'Continental socialism has lost its terrors for us'. Yet by 1887 Continental socialism was almost exclusively the theory heralded in the *Manifesto*. Thus, to a certain extent, the history of the *Manifesto* reflects the history of the modern working-class movement since 1848. At present it is doubtless the most widely circulated, the most international product of all socialist literature,

---

2 Proudhonists—Followers of Pierre Joseph Proudhon (1809-65), French founder of anarchist theory. His emphasis on decentralisation and the reduction of government power appealed to self-reliant peasant farmers and to artisans who owned their own workshops. Marx criticised Proudhon's artisanal utopia in *The Poverty of Philosophy*. Lassalleans—supporters of German socialist leader Ferdinand Lassalle (1825-64), whose political programme argued for universal suffrage and state-led economic reforms. Marx and Engels sharply criticised the Lassalleans' theory, strategy and tactics, especially for their effective support of the Prussian state of Bismarck.

the common programme of many millions of workers of all countries, from Siberia to California.

Nevertheless, when it appeared we could not have called it a socialist manifesto. In 1847 two kinds of people were considered socialists. On the one hand were the adherents of the various utopian systems, notably the Owenites in England and the Fourierists[3] in France, both of whom at that date had already dwindled to mere sects gradually dying out. On the other, the manifold types of social quacks who wanted to eliminate social abuses through their various universal panaceas and all kinds of patchwork, without hurting capital and profit in the least. In both cases, people who stood outside the labour movement and who looked for support rather to the 'educated' classes. The section of the working class, however, which demanded a radical reconstruction of society, convinced that mere political revolutions were not enough, then called itself communist. It was still a rough-hewn, only instinctive, and frequently somewhat crude communism. Yet it was powerful enough to bring into being two systems of utopian communism—in France the 'Icarian' communism of Cabet, and in Germany that of Weitling.[4] Socialism in 1847 signified a bourgeois movement, communism, a working-class movement. Socialism was, on the Continent at least, quite respectable, whereas communism was the very opposite. And since we were very decidedly of the opinion as early as then that 'the emancipation of the workers must be the act of the working class itself', we could have no hesitation as to which of the two names we should choose. Nor has it ever occurred to us since to repudiate it.

'Working men of all countries, unite!' But few voices responded when we proclaimed these words to the world 42 years ago, on the eve of the first Paris Revolution in which the proletariat came out with demands of its own. On 28 September 1864, however, the proletarians of most of the Western European countries joined hands in the International Working Men's Association of glorious memory. True, the International itself lived only nine years. But that the eternal

3   Owenites and Fourierists—followers of the utopian socialists Robert Owen and Charles Fourier, see p44

4   Wilhelm Weitling—Early leader of the German working class movement. Cabet's Icaria—see Engels' footnote p46

union of the proletarians of all countries created by it is still alive and lives stronger than ever, there is no better witness than this day. Because today, as I write these lines, the European and American proletariat is reviewing its fighting forces, mobilised for the first time, mobilised as *one* army, under *one* flag, for *one* immediate aim: the standard eight-hour working day, to be established by legal enactment, as proclaimed by the Geneva Congress of the International in 1866, and again by the Paris Workers' Congress in 1889. And today's spectacle will open the eyes of the capitalists and landlords of all countries to the fact that today the working men of all countries are united indeed.

If only Marx were still by my side to see this with his own eyes!

Frederick Engels
London, 1 May 1890

A spectre is haunting Europe—the spectre of communism. All the powers of old Europe have entered into a holy alliance to exorcise this spectre: Pope and Tsar, Metternich and Guizot, French Radicals and German police spies.

Where is the party in opposition that has not been decried as communistic by its opponents in power? Where the opposition that has not hurled back the branding reproach of communism, against the more advanced opposition parties, as well as against its reactionary adversaries?

Two things result from this fact:

1 Communism is already acknowledged by all European powers to be itself a power.

2 It is high time that communists should openly, in the face of the whole world, publish their views, their aims, their tendencies, and meet this nursery tale of the spectre of communism with a manifesto of the party itself.

To this end, communists of various nationalities have assembled in London, and sketched the following manifesto, to be published in the English, French, German, Italian, Flemish and Danish languages.

1

Bourgeois and proletarians[1]

The history of all hitherto existing society[2] is the history of class struggles.

Freeman and slave, patrician and plebeian, lord and serf, guild-master and journeyman,[3] in a word, oppressor and oppressed, stood in constant opposition to one another, carried on an uninterrupted, now hidden, now open fight, a fight that each time ended, either in a revolutionary reconstitution of society at large, or in the common ruin of the contending classes.

In the earlier epochs of history, we find almost everywhere a complicated arrangement of society into various orders, a manifold gradation of social rank. In ancient Rome we have patricians, knights, plebeians,

---

1   By bourgeoisie is meant the class of modern capitalists, owners of the means of social production and employers of wage labour. By proletariat, the class of modern wage-labourers who, having no means of production of their own, are reduced to selling their labour power in order to live. [Engels' note to the English edition of 1888]

2   That is, all written history. In 1847, the prehistory of society, the social organisation existing previous to recorded history, was all but unknown. Since then, Hathausen discovered common ownership of land in Russia, Maurer proved it to be the social foundation from which all Teutonic races started in history, and by and by village communities were found to be, or to have been the primitive form of society everywhere from India to Ireland. The inner organisation of this primitive communistic society was laid bare, in its typical form, by Morgan's crowning discovery of the true nature of the gens and its relation to the tribe. With the dissolution of these primeval communities society begins to be differentiated into separate and finally antagonistic classes. I have attempted to retrace this process of dissolution in: *The Origin of the Family, Private Property and the State*. [Engels' note to the English edition of 1888]

3   Guild-master and journeyman were different castes of medieval craftsmen.

slaves: in the Middle Ages, feudal lords, vassals, guild-masters, journeymen, apprentices, serfs; in almost all of these classes, again, subordinate gradations.

The modern bourgeois society that has sprouted from the ruins of feudal society has not done away with class antagonisms. It has but established new classes, new conditions of oppression, new forms of struggle in place of the old ones.

Our epoch, the epoch of the bourgeoisie, possesses, however, this distinctive feature: it has simplified the class antagonisms. Society as a whole is more and more splitting up into two great hostile camps, into two great classes directly facing each other: bourgeoisie and proletariat.

From the serfs of the Middle Ages sprang the chartered burghers of the earliest towns. From these burgesses the first elements of the bourgeoisie were developed.

The discovery of America, the rounding of the Cape, opened up fresh ground for the rising bourgeoisie. The East Indian and Chinese markets, the colonisation of America, trade with the colonies, the increase in the means of exchange and in commodities generally, gave to commerce, to navigation, to industry, an impulse never before known, and thereby, to the revolutionary element in the tottering feudal society, a rapid development.

The feudal system of industry, under which industrial production was monopolised by closed guilds, now no longer sufficed for the growing wants of the new markets. The manufacturing system took its place. The guild-masters were pushed on one side by the manufacturing middle class; division of labour between the different corporate guilds vanished in the face of division of labour in each single workshop.

Meantime the markets kept ever growing, the demand ever rising. Even manufacture no longer sufficed. Thereupon, steam and machinery revolutionised industrial production. The place of manufacture was taken by the giant, modern industry, the place of the industrial middle class, by industrial millionaires, the leaders of whole industrial armies, the modern bourgeois.

Modern industry has established the world market, for which the discovery of America paved the way. This market has given an immense development to commerce, to navigation, to communication by land. This development has, in its turn, reacted on the extension of industry;

and in proportion as industry, commerce, navigation, railways extended, in the same proportion the bourgeoisie developed, increased its capital, and pushed into the background every class handed down from the Middle Ages.

We see, therefore, how the modern bourgeoisie is itself the product of a long course of development, of a series of revolutions in the modes of production and of exchange.

Each step in the development of the bourgeoisie was accompanied by a corresponding political advance of that class. An oppressed class under the sway of the feudal nobility, an armed and self-governing association in the medieval commune; here independent urban republic (as in Italy and Germany), there taxable 'third estate' of the monarchy (as in France), afterwards, in the period of manufacture proper, serving either the semi-feudal or the absolute monarchy as a counterpoise against the nobility, and, in fact, cornerstone of the great monarchies in general, the bourgeoisie has at last, since the establishment of modern industry and of the world market, conquered for itself, in the modern representative state, exclusive political sway. The executive of the modern state is but a committee for managing the common affairs of the whole bourgeoisie.

The bourgeoisie, historically, has played a most revolutionary part.

The bourgeoisie, wherever it has got the upper hand, has put an end to all feudal, patriarchal, idyllic relations. It has pitilessly torn asunder the motley feudal ties that bound man to his 'natural superiors', and has left remaining no other nexus between man and man than naked self-interest, than callous 'cash payment'. It has drowned the most heavenly ecstasies of religious fervour, of chivalrous enthusiasm, of philistine sentimentalism, in the icy water of egotistical calculation. It has resolved personal worth into exchange value, and in place of the numberless indefeasible chartered freedoms, has set up that single, unconscionable freedom—Free Trade. In one word, for exploitation, veiled by religious and political illusions, it has substituted naked, shameless, direct, brutal exploitation.

The bourgeoisie has stripped of its halo every occupation hitherto honoured and looked up to with reverent awe. It has converted the physician, the lawyer, the priest, the poet, the man of science, into its paid wage-labourers.

The bourgeoisie has torn away from the family its sentimental veil, and has reduced the family relation to a mere money relation.

The bourgeoisie has disclosed how it came to pass that the brutal display of vigour in the Middle Ages, which reactionists so much admire, found its fitting complement in the most slothful indolence. It has been the first to show what man's activity can bring about. It has accomplished wonders far surpassing Egyptian pyramids, Roman aqueducts, and Gothic cathedrals; it has conducted expeditions that put in the shade all former exoduses of nations and crusades.

The bourgeoisie cannot exist without constantly revolutionising the instruments of production, and thereby the relations of production, and with them the whole relations of society. Conservation of the old modes of production in unaltered form, was, on the contrary, the first condition of existence for all earlier industrial classes. Constant revolutionising of production, uninterrupted disturbance of all social conditions, everlasting uncertainty and agitation distinguish the bourgeois epoch from all earlier ones. All fixed, fast-frozen relations, with their train of ancient and venerable prejudices and opinions are swept away, all new-formed ones become antiquated before they can ossify. All that is solid melts into air, all that is holy is profaned, and man is at last compelled to face with sober senses, his real conditions of life, and his relations with his kind.

The need of a constantly expanding market for its products chases the bourgeoisie over the whole surface of the globe. It must nestle everywhere, settle everywhere, establish connections everywhere.

The bourgeoisie has through its exploitation of the world market given a cosmopolitan character to production and consumption in every country. To the great chagrin of reactionists, it has drawn from under the feet of industry the national ground on which it stood. All old-established national industries have been destroyed or are daily being destroyed. They are dislodged by new industries, whose introduction becomes a life-and-death question for all civilised nations, by industries that no longer work up indigenous raw material, but raw material drawn from the remotest zones; industries whose products are consumed, not only at home, but in every quarter of the globe. In place of the old wants, satisfied by the productions of the country, we find new wants, requiring for their satisfaction the products of distant lands and climes. In place of the old local and national seclusion and self-sufficiency, we have intercourse in every direction, universal interdependence of nations. And as in material, so also in intellectual production. The intellectual creations of individual nations become common property. National one-sidedness and narrow-mindedness become more and more impossible, and from the numerous national and local literatures, there arises a world literature.

The bourgeoisie, by the rapid improvement of all instruments of production, by the immensely facilitated means of communication, draws all, even the most barbarian, nations into civilisation. The cheap prices of its commodities are the heavy artillery with which it batters down all Chinese walls, with which it forces the barbarians' intensely obstinate hatred of foreigners to capitulate. It compels all nations, on pain of extinction, to adopt the bourgeois mode of production; it compels them to introduce what it calls civilisation into their midst, ie, to become bourgeois themselves. In one word, it creates a world after its own image.

The bourgeoisie has subjected the country to the rule of the towns. It has created enormous cities, has greatly increased the urban population as compared with the rural and has thus rescued a considerable part of the population from the idiocy of rural life. Just as it has made the country dependent on the towns, so it has made barbarian and semi-barbarian countries dependent on the civilised ones, nations of peasants on nations of bourgeois, the East on the West.

The bourgeoisie keeps more and more doing away with the scattered state of the population, of the means of production, and of property. It has agglomerated population, centralised means of production, and has concentrated property in a few hands. The necessary consequence of this was political centralisation. Independent, or but loosely connected, provinces with separate interests, laws, governments and systems of taxation, became lumped together into one nation, with one government, one code of laws, one national class-interest, one frontier and one customs-tariff.

The bourgeoisie, during its rule of scarce 100 years, has created more massive and more colossal productive forces than have all preceding generations together. Subjection of nature's forces to man, machinery, application of chemistry to industry and agriculture, steam navigation, railways, electric telegraphs, clearing of whole continents for cultivation, canalisation of rivers, whole populations conjured out of the ground—what earlier century had even a presentiment that such productive forces slumbered in the lap of social labour?

We see then: the means of production and of exchange, on whose foundation the bourgeoisie built itself up, were generated in feudal society. At a certain stage in the development of these means of production and of exchange, the conditions under which feudal society produced and exchanged, the feudal organisation of agriculture and manufacturing industry, in one word, the feudal relations of property became no longer compatible with the already developed productive forces; they became so many fetters. They had to be burst asunder; they were burst asunder.

Into their place stepped free competition, accompanied by a social and political constitution adapted to it, and by the economical and political sway of the bourgeois class.

A similar movement is going on before our own eyes. Modern bourgeois society with its relations of production, of exchange and of property, a society that has conjured up such gigantic means of production and of exchange, is like the sorcerer, who is no longer able to control the powers of the nether world whom he has called up by his spells. For many a decade past the history of industry and commerce is but the history of the revolt of modern productive forces against modern conditions of production, against the property relations that are the conditions for the existence of the bourgeoisie and of its rule. It is enough to mention the commercial crises that by their periodical return put on its trial, each time more threateningly, the existence of the entire bourgeois society. In these crises a great part not only of the existing products, but also of the previously created productive forces, are periodically destroyed. In these crises there breaks out an epidemic that, in all earlier epochs, would have seemed an absurdity—the epidemic of overproduction. Society suddenly finds itself put back into a state of momentary barbarism; it appears as if a famine, a universal war of devastation had cut off the supply of every means of subsistence; industry and commerce seem to be destroyed; and why? Because there is too much civilisation, too much means of subsistence, too much industry, too much commerce. The productive forces at the disposal of society no longer tend to further the development of the conditions of bourgeois property; on the contrary, they have become too powerful for these conditions, by which they are fettered, and so soon as they overcome these fetters, they bring disorder into the whole of bourgeois society, endanger the existence of bourgeois property. The conditions of bourgeois society are too narrow to comprise the wealth created by them. And how does the bourgeoisie get over these crises? On the one hand by enforced destruction of a mass of productive forces; on the other, by the conquest of new markets, and by the more thorough exploitation of the old ones. That is to say, by paving the way for more extensive and more destructive crises, and by diminishing the means whereby crises are prevented.

The weapons with which the bourgeoisie felled feudalism to the ground are now turned against the bourgeoisie itself.

But not only has the bourgeoisie forged the weapons that bring death to itself; it has also called into existence the men who are to wield those weapons—the modern working class—the proletarians.

In proportion as the bourgeoisie, ie, capital is developed, in the same proportion is the proletariat, the modern working class, developed— a class of labourers, who live only so long as they find work, and who find work only so long as their labour increases capital. These labourers, who must sell themselves piecemeal, are a commodity, like every other article of commerce, and are consequently exposed to all the vicissitudes of competition, to all the fluctuations of the market.

Owing to the extensive use of machinery and to division of labour, the work of the proletarians has lost all individual character, and, consequently, all charm for the workman. He becomes an appendage of the machine, and it is only the most simple, most monotonous, and most easily acquired knack, that is required of him. Hence, the cost of production of a workman is restricted, almost entirely, to the means of subsistence that he requires for his maintenance, and for the propagation of his race. But the price of a commodity, and therefore also of labour, is equal to its cost of production. In proportion, therefore, as the repulsiveness of the work increases, the wage decreases. Nay more, in proportion as the use of machinery and division of labour increases, in the same proportion the burden of toil also increases, whether by prolongation of the working hours, by increase of the work exacted in a given time or by increased speed of the machinery, etc.

Modern industry has converted the little workshop of the patriarchal master into the great factory of the industrial capitalist. Masses of labourers, crowded into the factory, are organised like soldiers. As privates of the industrial army they are placed under the command of a perfect hierarchy of officers and sergeants. Not only are they slaves of the bourgeois class, and of the bourgeois state; they are daily and hourly enslaved by the machine, by the overlooker, and, above all, by the individual bourgeois manufacturer himself. The more openly this despotism proclaims gain to be its end and aim, the more petty, the more hateful and the more embittering it is.

The less the skill and exertion of strength implied in manual labour, in other words, the more modern industry becomes developed, the more is the labour of men superseded by that of women. Differences of age and sex have no longer any distinctive social validity for the working class. All are instruments of labour, more or less expensive to use, according to their age and sex.

No sooner is the exploitation of the labourer by the manufacturer, so far, at an end, that he receives his wages in cash, than he is set upon by the other portions of the bourgeoisie, the landlord, the shopkeeper, the pawnbroker, etc.

The lower strata of the middle class—the small tradespeople, shopkeepers, and retired tradesmen generally, the handicraftsmen and peasants—all these sink gradually into the proletariat, partly because their diminutive capital does not suffice for the scale on which modern industry is carried on, and is swamped in the competition with the large capitalists, partly because their specialised skill is rendered worthless by new methods of production. Thus the proletariat is recruited from all classes of the population.

The proletariat goes through various stages of development. With its birth begins its struggle with the bourgeoisie. At first the contest is carried on by individual labourers, then by the work-people of a factory, then by the operatives of one trade, in one locality, against the individual bourgeois who directly exploits them. They direct their attacks not against the bourgeois conditions of production, but against the instruments of production themselves; they destroy imported wares that compete with their labour, they smash to pieces machinery, they set factories ablaze, they seek to restore by force the vanished status of the workman of the Middle Ages.

At this stage the labourers still form an incoherent mass scattered over the whole country, and broken up by their mutual competition. If anywhere they unite to form more compact bodies, this is not yet the consequence of their own active union, but of the union of the bourgeoisie, which class, in order to attain its own political ends, is compelled to set the whole proletariat in motion, and is moreover yet, for a time, able to do so. At this stage, therefore, the proletarians do not fight their enemies, but the enemies of their enemies, the remnants of absolute monarchy, the landowners, the non-industrial bourgeois, the petit bourgeoisie. Thus the whole historical movement is concentrated in the hands of the bourgeoisie; every victory so obtained is a victory for the bourgeoisie.

But with the development of industry the proletariat not only increases in number; it becomes concentrated in greater masses, its strength grows, and it feels that strength more. The various interests and conditions of life within the ranks of the proletariat are more and more equalised, in proportion as machinery obliterates all distinctions of labour, and nearly everywhere reduces wages to the same low level. The growing competition among the bourgeois, and the resulting commercial crises, make the wages of the workers ever more fluctuating. The unceasing improvement of machinery, ever more rapidly developing, makes their livelihood more and more precarious; the collisions between individual workmen and individual bourgeois take more and more the character of collisions between two classes. Thereupon the workers begin to form combinations (trades unions) against the bourgeois; they club together in order to keep up the rate of wages; they found permanent associations in order to make provision beforehand for these occasional revolts. Here and there the contest breaks out into riots.

Now and then the workers are victorious, but only for a time. The real fruit of their battles lies, not in the immediate result, but in the ever-expanding union of the workers. This union is helped on by the improved means of communication that are created by modern industry and that place the workers of different localities in contact with one another. It was just this contact that was needed to centralise

21

the numerous local struggles, all of the same character, into one national struggle between classes. But every class struggle is a political struggle. And that union, to attain which the burghers of the Middle Ages, with their miserable highways, required centuries, the modern proletarians, thanks to railways, achieve in a few years.

This organisation of the proletarians into a class, and consequently into a political party, is continually being upset again by the competition between the workers themselves. But it ever rises up again, stronger, firmer, mightier. It compels legislative recognition of particular interests of the workers, by taking advantage of the divisions among the bourgeoisie itself. Thus the Ten Hours bill in England was carried.

Altogether collisions between the classes of the old society further, in many ways, the course of development of the proletariat. The bourgeoisie finds itself involved in a constant battle. At first with the aristocracy; later on, with those portions of the bourgeoisie itself, whose interests have become antagonistic to the progress of industry; at all times, with the bourgeoisie of foreign countries. In all these battles it sees itself compelled to appeal to the proletariat, to ask for its help, and thus, to drag it into the political arena. The bourgeoisie itself, therefore, supplies the proletariat with its own elements of political and general education, in other words, it furnishes the proletariat with weapons for fighting the bourgeoisie.

Further, as we have already seen, entire sections of the ruling classes are, by the advance of industry, precipitated into the proletariat, or are at least threatened in their conditions of existence. These also supply the proletariat with fresh elements of enlightenment and progress.

Finally, in times when the class struggle nears the decisive hour, the process of dissolution going on within the ruling class, in fact within the whole range of old society, assumes such a violent, glaring character, that a small section of the ruling class cuts itself adrift, and joins the revolutionary class, the class that holds the future in its hands. Just as, therefore, at an earlier period, a section of the nobility went over to the bourgeoisie, so now a portion of the bourgeoisie goes over to the proletariat, and in particular, a portion of the bourgeois ideologists, who have raised themselves to the level of comprehending theoretically the historical movement as a whole.

Of all the classes that stand face to face with the bourgeoisie today, the proletariat alone is a really revolutionary class. The other classes decay and finally disappear in the face of modern industry; the proletariat is its special and essential product.

The lower middle class, the small manufacturer, the shopkeeper, the artisan, the peasant, all these fight against the bourgeoisie, to save from extinction their existence as fractions of the middle class. They are therefore not revolutionary, but conservative. Nay more, they are reactionary, for they try to roll back the wheel of history. If by chance they are revolutionary, they are so only in view of their impending transfer into the proletariat, they thus defend not their present, but their future interests, they desert their own standpoint to place themselves at that of the proletariat.

The 'dangerous class', the social scum, that passively rotting mass thrown off by the lowest layers of old society may, here and there, be swept into the movement by a proletarian revolution; its conditions of life, however, prepare it far more for the part of a bribed tool of reactionary intrigue.

In the conditions of the proletariat, those of old society at large are already virtually swamped. The proletarian is without property; his relation to his wife and children has no longer anything in common with the bourgeois family relations; modern industrial labour, modern subjection to capital, the same in England as in France, in America as in Germany, has stripped him of every trace of national character. Law, morality, religion, are to him so many bourgeois prejudices, behind which lurk in ambush just as many bourgeois interests.

All the preceding classes that got the upper hand sought to fortify their already acquired status by subjecting society at large to their conditions of appropriation. The proletarians cannot become masters of the productive forces of society, except by abolishing their own previous mode of appropriation, and thereby also every other previous mode of appropriation. They have nothing of their own to secure and to fortify; their mission is to destroy all previous securities for, and insurances of, individual property.

All previous historical movements were movements of minorities, or in the interest of minorities. The proletarian movement is the self-conscious, independent movement of the immense majority, in the interest of the immense majority. The proletariat, the lowest stratum of our present society, cannot stir, cannot raise itself up, without the whole superincumbent strata of official society being sprung into the air.

Though not in substance, yet in form, the struggle of the proletariat with the bourgeoisie is at first a national struggle. The proletariat of each country must, of course, first of all settle matters with its own bourgeoisie.

In depicting the most general phases of the development of the proletariat, we traced the more or less veiled civil war, raging within existing society, up to the point where that war breaks out into open revolution, and where the violent overthrow of the bourgeoisie lays the foundation for the sway of the proletariat.

Hitherto, every form of society has been based, as we have already seen, on the antagonism of oppressing and oppressed classes. But in order to oppress a class, certain conditions must be assured to it under which it can, at least, continue its slavish existence. The serf, in the period of serfdom, raised himself to membership in the commune, just as the petit bourgeois, under the yoke of feudal absolutism, managed to develop into a bourgeois. The modern labourer, on the contrary, instead of rising with the progress of industry, sinks deeper and deeper below the conditions of existence of his own class. He becomes a pauper, and pauperism develops more rapidly than population and wealth. And here it becomes evident, that the bourgeoisie is unfit any longer to be the ruling class in society, and to impose its conditions of existence upon society as an overriding law. It is unfit to rule because it is incompetent to assure an existence to its slave within his slavery, because it cannot help letting him sink into such a state, that it has to feed him, instead of being fed by him. Society can no longer live under this bourgeoisie, in other words, its existence is no longer compatible with society.

The essential condition for the existence, and for the sway of the bourgeois class, is the formation and augmentation of capital; the condition for capital is wage labour. Wage labour rests exclusively on competition between the labourers. The advance of industry, whose involuntary promoter is the bourgeoisie, replaces the isolation of the labourers, due to competition, by their revolutionary combination, due to association. The development of modern industry, therefore, cuts from under its feet the very foundation on which the bourgeoisie produces and appropriates products. What the bourgeoisie, therefore, produces, above all, is its own grave-diggers. Its fall and the victory of the proletariat are equally inevitable.

2

Proletarians and communists

In what relation do the communists stand to the proletarians as a whole?

The communists do not form a separate party opposed to other working class parties.

They have no interests separate and apart from those of the proletariat as a whole.

They do not set up any sectarian principles of their own, by which to shape and mould the proletarian movement.

The communists are distinguished from the other working class parties by this only: 1) In the national struggles of the proletarians of the different countries, they point out and bring to the front the common interests of the entire proletariat, independently of all nationality. 2) In the various stages of development which the struggle of the working class against the bourgeoisie has to pass through, they always and everywhere represent the interests of the movement as a whole.

The communists, therefore, are on the one hand, practically, the most advanced and resolute section of the working class parties of every country, that section which pushes forward all others; on the other hand, theoretically, they have over the great mass of the proletariat the advantage of clearly understanding the line of march, the conditions, and the ultimate general results of the proletarian movement.

The immediate aim of the communists is the same as that of all the other proletarian parties: formation of the proletariat into a class, overthrow of the bourgeois supremacy, conquest of political power by the proletariat.

The theoretical conclusions of the communists are in no way based on ideas or principles that have been invented, or discovered, by this or that would-be universal reformer.

They merely express, in general terms, actual relations springing from an existing class struggle, from a historical movement going on under our very eyes. The abolition of existing property relations is not at all a distinctive feature of communism.

All property relations in the past have continually been subject to historical change consequent upon the change in historical conditions.

The French Revolution, for example, abolished feudal property in favour of bourgeois property.

The distinguishing feature of communism is not the abolition of property generally, but the abolition of bourgeois property. But modern bourgeois private property is the final and most complete expression of the system of producing and appropriating products, that is based on class antagonisms, on the exploitation of the many by the few.

In this sense, the theory of the communists may be summed up in the single sentence: abolition of private property.

We communists have been reproached with the desire of abolishing the right of personally acquiring property as the fruit of a man's own labour, which property is alleged to be the ground work of all personal freedom, activity and independence.

Hard-won, self-acquired, self-earned property! Do you mean the property of the petty artisan and of the small peasant, a form of property that preceded the bourgeois form? There is no need to abolish that; the development of industry has to a great extent already destroyed it, and is still destroying it daily.

Or do you mean modern bourgeois private property?

But does wage labour create any property for the labourer? Not a bit. It creates capital, ie, that kind of property which exploits wage labour, and which cannot increase except upon condition of begetting a new supply of wage labour for fresh exploitation. Property, in its present form, is based on the antagonism of capital and wage labour. Let us examine both sides of this antagonism.

To be a capitalist is to have not only a purely personal but a social *status* in production. Capital is a collective product, and only by the united action of many members, nay, in the last resort, only by the united action of all members of society, can it be set in motion.

Capital is, therefore, not a personal, it is a social power.

When, therefore, capital is converted into common property, into the property of all members of society, personal property is not thereby transformed into social property. It is only the social character of the property that is changed. It loses its class character.

Let us now take wage labour.

The average price of wage labour is the minimum wage, ie, that quantum of the means of subsistence which is absolutely requisite to keep the labourer in bare existence as a labourer. What, therefore, the wage-labourer appropriates by means of his labour, merely suffices to prolong and reproduce a bare existence. We by no means intend to abolish this personal appropriation of the products of labour, an appropriation that is made for the maintenance and reproduction of human life, and that leaves no surplus wherewith to command the labour of others. All that we want to do away with is the miserable character of this appropriation, under which the labourer lives merely to increase capital, and is allowed to live only in so far as the interest of the ruling class requires it.

In bourgeois society, living labour is but a means to increase accumulated labour. In communist society, accumulated labour is but a means to widen, to enrich, to promote the existence of the labourer.

In bourgeois society, therefore, the past dominates the present; in communist society, the present dominates the past. In bourgeois society capital is independent and has individuality, while the living person is dependent and has no individuality.

And the abolition of this state of things is called by the bourgeois, abolition of individuality and freedom! And rightly so. The abolition of bourgeois individuality, bourgeois independence, and bourgeois freedom is undoubtedly aimed at.

By freedom is meant, under the present bourgeois conditions of production, free trade, free selling and buying.

But if selling and buying disappears, free selling and buying disappears also. This talk about free selling and buying, and all the other 'brave words' of our bourgeoisie about freedom in general, have a meaning, if any, only in contrast with restricted selling and buying, with the fettered traders of the Middle Ages, but have no meaning when opposed to the communistic abolition of buying and selling, of the bourgeois conditions of production, and of the bourgeoisie itself.

You are horrified at our intending to do away with private property. But in your existing society, private property is already done away with for nine-tenths of the population; its existence for the few is solely due to its non-existence in the hands of those nine-tenths. You reproach us, therefore, with intending to do away with a form of property the necessary condition for whose existence is the non-existence of any property for the immense majority of society.

In one word, you reproach us with intending to do away with your property. Precisely so; that is just what we intend.

From the moment when labour can no longer be converted into capital, money, or rent, into a social power capable of being monopolised, ie, from the moment when individual property can no longer be transformed into bourgeois property, into capital, from that moment, you say, individuality vanishes.

You must, therefore, confess that by 'individual' you mean no other person than the bourgeois, than the middle class owner of property. This person must, indeed, be swept out of the way, and made impossible.

Communism deprives no man of the power to appropriate the products of society; all that it does is to deprive him of the power to subjugate the labour of others by means of such appropriation.

It has been objected that upon the abolition of private property all work will cease, and universal laziness will overtake us.

According to this, bourgeois society ought long ago to have gone to the dogs through sheer idleness; for those of its members who work, acquire nothing, and those who acquire anything, do not work. The whole of this objection is but another expression of the tautology: that there can no longer be any wage labour when there is no longer any capital.

All objections urged against the communistic mode of producing and appropriating material products, have, in the same way, been urged against the communistic modes of producing and appropriating intellectual products. Just as, to the bourgeois, the disappearance of class property is the disappearance of production itself, so the disappearance of class culture is to him identical with the disappearance of all culture.

That culture, the loss of which he laments, is, for the enormous majority, a mere training to act as a machine.

But don't wrangle with us so long as you apply, to our intended abolition of bourgeois property, the standard of your bourgeois notions of freedom, culture, law, etc. Your very ideas are but the outgrowth of the conditions of your bourgeois production and bourgeois property, just as your jurisprudence is but the will of your class made into a law for all, a will, whose essential character and direction are determined by the economical conditions of existence of your class.

The selfish misconception that induces you to transform into eternal laws of nature and of reason, the social forms springing from your present mode of production and form of property—historical relations that rise and disappear in the progress of production—this misconception you share with every ruling class that has preceded you. What you see clearly in the case of ancient property, what you admit in the case of feudal property, you are of course forbidden to admit in the case of your own bourgeois form of property.

Abolition of the family! Even the most radical flare up at this infamous proposal of the communists.

On what foundation is the present family, the bourgeois family, based? On capital, on private gain. In its completely developed form this family exists only among the bourgeoisie. But this state of things finds its complement in the practical absence of the family among the proletarians, and in public prostitution.

The bourgeois family will vanish as a matter of course when its complement vanishes, and both will vanish with the vanishing of capital.

Do you charge us with wanting to stop the exploitation of children by their parents? To this crime we plead guilty.

But, you will say, we destroy the most hallowed of relations, when we replace home education by social.

And your education! Is not that also social, and determined by the social conditions under which you educate, by the intervention, direct or indirect, of society, by means of schools, etc? The communists have not invented the intervention of society in education; they do but seek to alter the character of that intervention, and to rescue education from the influence of the ruling class.

The bourgeois claptrap about the family and education, about the hallowed co-relation of parent and child, becomes all the more disgusting, the more, by the action of modern industry, all family ties among the proletarians are torn asunder, and their children transformed into simple articles of commerce and instruments of labour.

But you communists would introduce community of women, screams the whole bourgeoisie in chorus.

The bourgeois sees in his wife a mere instrument of production. He hears that the instruments of production are to be exploited in common, and, naturally, can come to no other conclusion than that the lot of being common to all will likewise fall to the women.

He has not even a suspicion that the real point aimed at is to do away with the status of women as mere instruments of production.

For the rest, nothing is more ridiculous than the virtuous indignation of our bourgeois at the community of women which, they pretend, is to be openly and officially established by the communists. The communists have no need to introduce community of women; it has existed almost from time immemorial.

Our bourgeois, not content with having the wives and daughters of their proletarians at their disposal, not to speak of common prostitutes, take the greatest pleasure in seducing each other's wives.

Bourgeois marriage is in reality a system of wives in common and thus, at the most, what the communists might possibly be reproached with, is that they desire to introduce, in substitution for a hypocritically concealed, an openly legalised community of women. For the rest, it is self-evident that the abolition of the present system of production must bring with it the abolition of the community of women springing from that system, ie, of prostitution both public and private.

The communists are further reproached with desiring to abolish countries and nationality.

The working men have no country. We cannot take from them what they have not got. Since the proletariat must first of all acquire political supremacy, must rise to be the leading class of the nation, must constitute itself *the* nation, it is, so far, itself national, though not in the bourgeois sense of the word.

National differences and antagonisms between peoples are daily more and more vanishing, owing to the development of the bourgeoisie, to freedom of commerce, to the world market, to uniformity in the mode of production and in the conditions of life corresponding thereto.

The supremacy of the proletariat will cause them to vanish still faster. United action, of the leading civilised countries at least, is one of the first conditions for the emancipation of the proletariat.

In proportion as the exploitation of one individual by another is put an end to, the exploitation of one nation by another will also be put an end to. In proportion as the antagonism between classes within the nation vanishes, the hostility of one nation to another will come to an end.

The charges against communism made from a religious, a philosophical, and, generally, from an ideological standpoint, are not deserving of serious examination.

Does it require deep intuition to comprehend that man's ideas, views and conceptions, in one word, man's consciousness, changes with every change in the conditions of his material existence, in his social relations and in his social life?

What else does the history of ideas prove, than that intellectual production changes in character in proportion as material production is changed? The ruling ideas of each age have ever been the ideas of its ruling class.

When people speak of ideas that revolutionise society, they do but express the fact, that within the old society, the elements of a new one have been created, and that the dissolution of the old ideas keeps even pace with the dissolution of the old conditions of existence.

When the ancient world was in its last throes, the ancient religions were overcome by Christianity. When Christian ideas succumbed in the eighteenth century to rationalist ideas, feudal society fought its death battle with the then revolutionary bourgeoisie. The ideas of religious liberty and freedom of conscience, merely gave expression to the sway of free competition within the domain of knowledge.

'Undoubtedly', it will be said, 'religious, moral, philosophical and juridical ideas have been modified in the course of historical development. But religion, morality, philosophy, political science, and law, constantly survived this change.

'There are, besides, eternal truths, such as Freedom, Justice, etc, that are common to all states of society. But communism abolishes eternal truths, it abolishes all religion, and all morality, instead of constituting them on a new basis; it therefore acts in contradiction to all past historical experience.'

What does this accusation reduce itself to? The history of all past society has consisted in the development of class antagonisms, antagonisms that assumed different forms at different epochs.

But whatever form they may have taken, one fact is common to all past ages, viz, the exploitation of one part of society by the other. No wonder, then, that the social consciousness of past ages, despite all the multiplicity and variety it displays, moves within certain common forms, or general ideas, which cannot completely vanish except with the total disappearance of class antagonisms.

The communist revolution is the most radical rupture with traditional property relations; no wonder that its development involves the most radical rupture with traditional ideas.

But let us have done with the bourgeois objections to communism.

We have seen above, that the first step in the revolution by the working class, is to raise the proletariat to the position of ruling class, to win the battle of democracy.

The proletariat will use its political supremacy to wrest, by degrees, all capital from the bourgeoisie, to centralise all instruments of production in the hands of the state, ie, of the proletariat organised as the ruling class; and to increase the total of productive forces as rapidly as possible.

Of course, in the beginning, this cannot be effected except by means of despotic inroads on the rights of property, and on the conditions of bourgeois production; by means of measures, therefore, which appear economically insufficient and untenable, but which, in the course of the movement, outstrip themselves, necessitate further inroads upon the old social order, and are unavoidable as a means of entirely revolutionising the mode of production.

These measures will of course be different in different countries.

Nevertheless, in the most advanced countries, the following will be pretty generally applicable:

1 Abolition of property in land and application of all rents of land to public purposes.

2 A heavy progressive or graduated income tax.

3 Abolition of all right of inheritance.

4 Confiscation of the property of all emigrants and rebels.

5 Centralisation of credit in the hands of the state, by means of a national bank with state capital and an exclusive monopoly.

6 Centralisation of the means of communication and transport in the hands of the state.

7 Extension of factories and instruments of production owned by the state; the bringing into cultivation of wastelands, and the improvement of the soil generally in accordance with a common plan.

8 Equal liability of all to labour. Establishment of industrial armies, especially for agriculture.

9 Combination of agriculture with manufacturing industries; gradual abolition of the distinction between town and country, by a more equable distribution of the population over the country.

10 Free education for all children in public schools. Abolition of children's factory labour in its present form. Combination of education with industrial production, etc, etc.

When, in the course of development, class distinctions have disappeared, and all production has been concentrated in the whole nation, the public power will lose its political character. Political power, properly so called, is merely the organised power of one class for oppressing another. If the proletariat during its contest with the bourgeoisie is compelled, by the force of circumstances, to organise itself as a class, if, by means of a revolution, it makes itself the ruling class, and, as such, sweeps away by force the old conditions of production, then it will, along with these conditions, have swept away the conditions for the existence of class antagonisms and of classes generally, and will thereby have abolished its own supremacy as a class.

In place of the old bourgeois society, with its classes and class antagonisms, we shall have an association, in which the free development of each is the condition for the free development of all.

3

Socialist and communist literature

I Reactionary socialism

a) Feudal socialism

Owing to their historical position, it became the vocation of the aristocracies of France and England to write pamphlets against modern bourgeois society. In the French revolution of July 1830, and in the English reform agitation, these aristocracies again succumbed to the hateful upstart.[1] Thenceforth, a serious political contest was altogether out of the question. A literary battle alone remained possible. But even in the domain of literature the old cries of the restoration period[2] had become impossible.

In order to arouse sympathy, the aristocracy were obliged to lose sight, apparently, of their own interests, and to formulate their indictment against the bourgeoisie in the interest of the exploited working class alone. Thus the aristocracy took their revenge by singing lampoons on their new master, and whispering in his ears sinister prophecies of coming catastrophe.

In this way arose feudal socialism: half lamentation, half lampoon; half echo of the past, half menace of the future; at times, by its bitter, witty and incisive criticism, striking the bourgeoisie to the very heart's core; but always ludicrous in its effect, through total incapacity to comprehend the march of modern history.

The aristocracy, in order to rally the people to them, waved the

---

1   In July 1830 the Legitimist Charles X was overthrown and replaced by the bourgeois monarch Louis Philippe. The English reform act of 1832 extended the franchise.

2   *Not* the English Restoration 1660 to 1689, but the French Restoration 1814 to 1830. [Engels' note to the English edition of 1888]

proletarian alms-bag in front for a banner. But the people, so often as it joined them, saw on their hindquarters the old feudal coats of arms, and deserted with loud and irreverent laughter.

One section of the French Legitimists and 'Young England' exhibited this spectacle.

In pointing out that their mode of exploitation was different to that of the bourgeoisie, the feudalists forget that they exploited under circumstances and conditions that were quite different, and that are now antiquated. In showing that, under their rule, the modern proletariat never existed, they forget that the modern bourgeoisie is the necessary offspring of their own form of society.

For the rest, so little do they conceal the reactionary character of their criticism that their chief accusation against the bourgeoisie amounts to this, that under the bourgeois regime a class is being developed, which is destined to cut up root and branch the old order of society.

What they upbraid the bourgeoisie with is not so much that it creates a proletariat, as that it creates a *revolutionary* proletariat.

In political practice, therefore, they join in all coercive measures against the working class; and in ordinary life, despite their high-falutin phrases, they stoop to pick up the golden apples dropped from the tree of industry, and to barter truth, love, and honour for traffic in wool, beetroot-sugar and potato spirits.[3]

As the parson has ever gone hand in hand with the landlord, so has clerical socialism with feudal socialism.

Nothing is easier than to give Christian ascetism a socialist tinge. Has not Christianity declaimed against private property, against marriage, against the state? Has it not preached in the place of these, charity and poverty, celibacy and mortification of the flesh, monastic life and Mother Church? Christian socialism is but the holy water with which the priest consecrates the heart-burnings of the aristocrat.

---

3   This applies chiefly to Germany where the landed aristocracy and squirearchy have large portions of their estates cultivated for their own account by stewards, and are, moreover, extensive beetroot-sugar manufacturers and distillers of potato spirits. The wealthier British aristocracy are, as yet, rather above that; but they, too, know how to make up for declining rents by lending their names to floaters of more or less shady joint-stock companies. [Engels' note to the English edition of 1888]

b) Petit-bourgeois socialism

The feudal aristocracy was not the only class that was ruined by the bourgeoisie, not the only class whose conditions of existence pined and perished in the atmosphere of modern bourgeois society. The medieval burgesses and the small peasant proprietors were the precursors of the modern bourgeoisie. In those countries which are but little developed, industrially and commercially, these two classes still vegetate side by side with the rising bourgeoisie.

In countries where modern civilisation has become fully developed, a new class of petit bourgeois has been formed, fluctuating between proletariat and bourgeoisie and ever renewing itself as a supplementary part of bourgeois society. The individual members of this class, however, are being constantly hurled down into the proletariat by the action of competition, and, as modern industry develops, they even see the moment approaching when they will completely disappear as an independent section of modern society, to be replaced, in manufacture, agriculture and commerce, by overlookers, bailiffs and shopmen.

In countries like France, where the peasants constitute far more than half of the population, it was natural that writers who sided with the proletariat against the bourgeoisie, should use, in their criticism of the bourgeois regime, the standard of the peasant and petit bourgeois, and from the standpoint of these intermediate classes should take up the cudgels for the working class. Thus arose petit-bourgeois socialism. Sismondi was the head of this school, not only in France but also in England.[4]

This school of socialism dissected with great acuteness the contradictions in the conditions of modern production. It laid bare the hypocritical apologies of economists. It proved, incontrovertibly, the disastrous effects of machinery and division of labour; the concentration of capital and land in a few hands; over-production and crises; it pointed out the inevitable ruin of the petit bourgeois and peasant, the misery of the proletariat, the anarchy in production, the crying inequalities in the distribution of wealth, the industrial war of extermination between nations, the dissolution of old moral bonds, of the old family relations, of the old nationalities.

---

4   Jean Charles Léonard Simonde de Sismondi (1773-1842)—Swiss economist and historian

In its positive aims, however, this form of socialism aspires either to restoring the old means of production and of exchange, and with them the old property relations, and the old society, or to cramping the modern means of production and of exchange, within the framework of the old property relations that have been, and were bound to be, exploded by those means. In either case, it is both reactionary and utopian.

Its last words are: corporate guilds for manufacture; patriarchal relations in agriculture.

Ultimately, when stubborn historical facts had dispersed all intoxicating effects of self-deception, this form of socialism ended in a miserable fit of the blues.

c) German, or 'True', socialism

The socialist and communist literature of France, a literature that originated under the pressure of a bourgeoisie in power, and that was the expression of the struggle against this power, was introduced into Germany at a time when the bourgeoisie, in that country, had just begun its contest with feudal absolutism.

German philosophers, would-be philosophers, and *beaux esprits*, eagerly seized on this literature, only forgetting, that when these writings migrated from France into Germany, French social conditions had not migrated along with them. In contact with German social conditions, this French literature lost all its immediate practical significance, and assumed a purely literary aspect. Thus, to the German philosophers of the eighteenth century, the demands of the first French Revolution were nothing more than the demands of 'Practical Reason' in general, and the utterance of the will of the revolutionary French bourgeoisie signified in their eyes the laws of pure Will, of Will as it was bound to be, of true human Will generally.

The work of the German *literati* consisted solely in bringing the new French ideas into harmony with their ancient philosophical conscience, or rather, in annexing the French ideas without deserting their own philosophic point of view.

This annexation took place in the same way in which a foreign language is appropriated, namely, by translation.

It is well known how the monks wrote silly lives of Catholic saints *over* the manuscripts on which the classical works of ancient hea-thendom had been written. The German *literati* reversed this process with the profane French literature. They wrote their philosophical non-sense beneath the French original. For instance, beneath the French criticism of the economic functions of money, they wrote 'Alienation of Humanity', and beneath the French criticism of the bourgeois State they wrote, 'Dethronement of the Category of the General', and so forth.

The introduction of these philosophical phrases at the back of the French historical criticisms they dubbed 'Philosophy of Action', 'True Socialism', 'German Science of Socialism', 'Philosophical Foundation of Socialism', and so on.

The French socialist and communist literature was thus completely emasculated. And, since it ceased in the hands of the German to express the struggle of one class with the other, he felt conscious of having overcome 'French one-sidedness' and of representing, not true requirements, but the requirements of Truth; not the interests of the proletariat, but the interests of Human Nature, of Man in general, who belongs to no class, has no reality, who exists only in the misty realm of philosophical fantasy.

This German socialism, which took its schoolboy task so seriously and solemnly, and extolled its poor stock-in-trade in such mountebank fashion, meanwhile gradually lost its pedantic innocence.

The fight of the German, and, especially of the Prussian bourgeoisie, against feudal aristocracy and absolute monarchy, in other words, the liberal movement, became more earnest.

By this, the long wished-for opportunity was offered to 'True' Socialism of confronting the political movement with the socialist demands, of hurling the traditional anathemas against liberalism, against representative government, against bourgeois competition, bourgeois freedom of the press, bourgeois legislation, bourgeois liberty and equality, and of preaching to the masses that they had nothing to gain, and everything to lose, by this bourgeois movement. German socialism forgot, in the nick of time, that the French criticism, whose silly echo it was, presupposed the existence of modern bourgeois society, with its corresponding economic conditions of existence, and the political constitution adapted thereto, the very things whose attainment was the object of the pending struggle in Germany.

To the absolute governments, with their following of parsons, professors, country squires and officials, it served as a welcome scarecrow against the threatening bourgeoisie.

It was a sweet finish after the bitter pills of floggings and bullets with which these same governments, just at that time, dosed the German working class risings.

While this 'True' Socialism thus served the governments as a weapon for fighting the German bourgeoisie, it, at the same time, directly represented a reactionary interest, the interest of the German philistines. In Germany the petit-bourgeois class, a relic of the sixteenth century, and since then constantly cropping up again under various forms, is the real social basis of the existing state of things.

To preserve this class is to preserve the existing state of things in Germany. The industrial and political supremacy of the bourgeoisie threatens it with certain destruction; on the one hand, from the concentration of capital; on the other, from the rise of a revolutionary proletariat. 'True' Socialism appeared to kill these two birds with one stone. It spread like an epidemic.

The robe of speculative cobwebs, embroidered with flowers of rhetoric, steeped in the dew of sickly sentiment, this transcendental robe in which the German socialists wrapped their sorry 'eternal truths', all skin and bone, served to wonderfully increase the sale of their goods among such a public.

And on its part, German socialism recognised, more and more, its own calling as the bombastic representative of the petit-bourgeois philistine.

It proclaimed the German nation to be the model nation, and the German petty philistine to be the typical man. To every villainous meanness of this model man it gave a hidden, higher, socialistic interpretation, the exact contrary of its real character. It went to the extreme length of directly opposing the 'brutally destructive' tendency of communism, and of proclaiming its supreme and impartial contempt of all class struggles. With very few exceptions, all the so-called socialist and communist publications that now (1847) circulate in Germany belong to the domain of this foul and enervating literature.

II Conservative, or bourgeois, socialism

A part of the bourgeoisie is desirous of redressing social grievances, in order to secure the continued existence of bourgeois society.

To this section belong economists, philanthropists, humanitarians, improvers of the condition of the working class, organisers of charity, members of societies for the prevention of cruelty to animals, temperance fanatics, hole-and-corner reformers of every imaginable kind. This form of socialism has, moreover, been worked out into complete systems.

We may cite Proudhon's *Philosophie de la Misère* as an example of this form.

The socialistic bourgeois want all the advantages of modern social conditions without the struggles and dangers necessarily resulting therefrom. They desire the existing state of society minus its revolutionary and disintegrating elements. They wish for a bourgeoisie without a proletariat. The bourgeoisie naturally conceives the world in which it is supreme to be the best; and bourgeois socialism develops this comfortable conception into various more or less complete systems. In requiring the proletariat to carry out such a system, and thereby to march straightaway into the social New Jerusalem, it but requires in reality, that the proletariat should remain within the bounds of existing society, but should cast away all its hateful ideas concerning the bourgeoisie.

A second and more practical, but less systematic, form of this socialism sought to depreciate every revolutionary movement in the eyes of the working class, by showing that no mere political reform, but only a change in the material conditions of existence, in economical relations, could be of any advantage to them. By changes in the material conditions of existence, this form of socialism, however, by no means understands abolition of the bourgeois relations of production, an abolition that can be effected only by a revolution, but administrative reforms, based on the continued existence of these relations; reforms, therefore, that in no respect affect the relations between capital and labour, but, at the best, lessen the cost, and simplify the administrative work, of bourgeois government.

Bourgeois socialism attains adequate expression, when, and only when, it becomes a mere figure of speech.

Free trade: for the benefit of the working class. Protective duties: for the benefit of the working class. Prison reform: for the benefit of the working class. This is the last word and the only seriously meant word of bourgeois socialism.

It is summed up in the phrase: the bourgeois is a bourgeois—for the benefit of the working class.

III Critical-utopian socialism and communism

We do not here refer to that literature which, in every great modern revolution, has always given voice to the demands of the proletariat, such as the writings of Babeuf and others.[5]

The first direct attempts of the proletariat to attain its own ends, made in times of universal excitement, when feudal society was being overthrown, these attempts necessarily failed, owing to the then undeveloped state of the proletariat, as well as to the absence of the economic conditions for its emancipation, conditions that had yet to be produced, and could be produced by the impending bourgeois epoch alone. The revolutionary literature that accompanied these first movements of the proletariat had necessarily a reactionary character. It inculcated universal asceticism and social levelling in its crudest form.

The socialist and communist systems properly so called, those of Saint-Simon, Fourier, Owen and others,[6] spring into existence in the early undeveloped period, described above, of the struggle between proletariat and bourgeoisie (see Section 1, 'Bourgeois and proletarians').

The founders of these systems see, indeed, the class antagonisms, as well as the action of the decomposing elements in the prevailing form of society. But the proletariat, as yet in its infancy, offers to them the spectacle of a class without any historical initiative or any independent political movement.

---

5   Gracchus Babeuf (1760-97)—French revolutionary and utopian communist. In May 1796 he led an insurrection, 'The Conspiracy of Equals', based on a small group of dedicated revolutionaries, against the Directorate which then ruled France. He failed and was executed.

6   Henri Saint-Simon (1760-1825), Charles Fourier (1772-1837), Robert Owen (1771-1858)—for Marx and Engels' assessment of their historic significance see Engels' *Socialism: Scientific and Utopian*, Junius Publications, 1995.

Since the development of class antagonism keeps even pace with the development of industry, the economic situation, as they find it, does not as yet offer to them the material conditions for the emancipation of the proletariat. They therefore search after a new social science, after new social laws, that are to create these conditions.

Historical action is to yield to their personal inventive action, historically created conditions of emancipation to fantastic ones, and the gradual, spontaneous class organisation of the proletariat to an organisation of society specially contrived by these inventors. Future history resolves itself, in their eyes, into the propaganda and the practical carrying out of their social plans.

In the formation of their plans they are conscious of caring chiefly for the interests of the working class, as being the most suffering class. Only from the point of view of being the most suffering class does the proletariat exist for them.

The undeveloped state of the class struggle, as well as their own surroundings, causes socialists of this kind to consider themselves far superior to all class antagonisms. They want to improve the condition of every member of society, even that of the most favoured. Hence, they habitually appeal to society at large, without distinction of class; nay, by preference, to the ruling class. For how can people, when once they understand their system, fail to see in it the best possible plan of the best possible state of society?

Hence, they reject all political, and especially all revolutionary, action; they wish to attain their ends by peaceful means, and endeavour, by small experiments, necessarily doomed to failure, and by the force of example, to pave the way for the new social Gospel.

Such fantastic pictures of future society, painted at a time when the proletariat is still in a very undeveloped state and has but a fantastic conception of its own position correspond with the first instinctive yearnings of that class for a general reconstruction of society.

But these socialist and communist publications contain also a critical element. They attack every principle of existing society. Hence they are full of the most valuable materials for the enlightenment of the working class. The practical measures proposed in them—such as the abolition of the distinction between town and country, of the family, of the carrying on of industries for the account of private individuals, and of the wage system, the proclamation of social harmony, the conversion of the functions of the state into a mere superintendence of production, all these proposals point solely to the disappearance of class antagonisms which were, at that time, only just cropping up, and which, in these publications, are recognised in their earliest indistinct and undefined forms only. These proposals, therefore, are of a purely utopian character.

The significance of critical-utopian socialism and communism bears an inverse relation to historical development. In proportion as the modern class struggle develops and takes definite shape, this fantastic standing apart from the contest, these fantastic attacks on it, lose all practical value and all theoretical justification. Therefore, although the originators of these systems were, in many respects, revolutionary, their disciples have, in every case, formed mere reactionary sects. They hold fast by the original views of their masters, in opposition to the progressive historical development of the proletariat. They, therefore, endeavour, and that consistently, to deaden the class struggle and to reconcile the class antagonisms. They still dream of experimental realisation of their social utopias, of founding isolated 'phalanstères', of establishing 'Home Colonies', of setting up a 'Little Icaria'[7]—duodecimo editions of the New Jerusalem—and to realise all these castles in the air, they are compelled to appeal to the feelings and purses of the bourgeois. By degrees they sink into the category of the reactionary conservative socialists depicted above, differing from these only by more systematic pedantry, and by their fanatical and superstitious belief in the miraculous effects of their social science.

They, therefore, violently oppose all political action on the part of the working class; such action, according to them, can only result from blind unbelief in the new Gospel.

The Owenites in England, and the Fourierists in France, respectively oppose the Chartists and the *Réformistes*.[8]

---

7   'Home colonies' were what Owen called his communist model societies. *Phalanstères* was the name of the public palaces planned by Fourier. Icaria was the name given to the utopian land of fancy, whose communist institutions Cabet portrayed. [Engels' note to the German edition of 1890]

8   Supporters of the newspaper *La Réforme*, which was published in Paris from 1843 to 1850.

4

Position of the communists in relation to the various existing opposition parties

Section 2 has made clear the relations of the communists to the existing working class parties, such as the Chartists in England and the Agrarian Reformers in America.

The communists fight for the attainment of the immediate aims, for the enforcement of the momentary interests of the working class; but in the movement of the present, they also represent and take care of the future of that movement. In France the communists ally themselves with the Social-Democrats,[1] against the conservative and radical bourgeoisie, reserving, however, the right to take up a critical position in regard to phrases and illusions traditionally handed down from the Great Revolution.

In Switzerland they support the Radicals, without losing sight of the fact that this party consists of antagonistic elements, partly of Democratic Socialists, in the French sense, partly of radical bourgeois.

In Poland they support the party that insists on an agrarian revolution as the prime condition for national emancipation, that party which fomented the insurrection of Cracow in 1846.

In Germany they fight with the bourgeoisie whenever it acts in

---

1   The party then represented in parliament by Ledru-Rollin, in literature by Louis Blanc, in the daily press by the *Reforme*. The name of Social-Democracy signified, with these its inventors, a section of the Democratic or Republican party more or less tinged with socialism. [Engels' note to the English edition of 1888]

a revolutionary way, against the absolute monarchy, the feudal squirearchy, and the petit bourgeoisie.

But they never cease, for a single instant, to instil into the working class the clearest possible recognition of the hostile antagonism between bourgeoisie and proletariat, in order that the German workers may straightway use, as so many weapons against the bourgeoisie, the social and political conditions that the bourgeoisie must necessarily introduce along with its supremacy, and in order that, after the fall of the reactionary classes in Germany, the fight against the bourgeoisie itself may immediately begin.

The communists turn their attention chiefly to Germany, because that country is on the eve of a bourgeois revolution that is bound to be carried out under more advanced conditions of European civilisation, and with a much more developed proletariat, than that of England was in the seventeenth, and of France in the eighteenth century, and because the bourgeois revolution in Germany will be but the prelude to an immediately following proletarian revolution.

In short, the communists everywhere support every revolutionary movement against the existing social and political order of things.

In all these movements they bring to the front, as the leading question in each, the property question, no matter what its degree of development at the time.

Finally, they labour everywhere for the union and agreement of the democratic parties of all countries.

The communists disdain to conceal their views and aims. They openly declare that their ends can be attained only by the forcible over-throw of all existing social conditions. Let the ruling classes tremble at a communistic revolution. The proletarians have nothing to lose but their chains. They have a world to win.

WORKING MEN OF ALL COUNTRIES, UNITE!